Animal Survival

ANIMALS
AND THE QUEST
FOR FOOD

Michel Barré

Gareth Stevens Publishing
MILWAUKEE

— The author would particularly like to thank Jack Guichard and Maurice Berteloot for the encouragement, critiques, and advice that they gave during the writing of this book.

The editor would like to extend special thanks to Jan W. Rafert, Curator of Primates and Small Mammals, Milwaukee County Zoo, Milwaukee, Wisconsin, for his kind and professional help with the information in this book.

For a free color catalog describing Gareth Stevens' list of high-quality books and multimedia programs, call 1-800-542-2595 (USA) or 1-800-461-9120 (Canada). Gareth Stevens Publishing's Fax: (414) 225-0377. See our catalog, too, on the World Wide Web: http://gsinc.com

Library of Congress Cataloging-in-Publication Data

Barré, Michel, 1928-
   [Comment se nourrissent les animaux? English]
   Animals and the quest for food / by Michel Barré.
     p. cm. — (Animal survival)
   Includes bibliographical references (p. 47) and index.
   Summary: Discusses some of the ways animals obtain, eat, and
digest food.
   ISBN 0-8368-2079-7 (lib. bdg.)
   1. Animals—Food—Juvenile literature. 2. Food chains (Ecology)—
Juvenile literature. [1. Animals—Food habits.] I. Title. II. Series:
Barré, Michel, 1928- Animal survival.
QL756.5.B3713 1998
591.5'3—dc21   97-40157

This North American edition first published in 1998 by
Gareth Stevens Publishing
1555 North RiverCenter Drive, Suite 201
Milwaukee, Wisconsin 53212 USA

This U.S. edition © 1998 by Gareth Stevens, Inc. Original © 1994 by Éditions MANGO-Éditions PEMF, under the French title *Comment se nourrissent les animaux?*. Additional end matter © 1998 by Gareth Stevens, Inc.

Translated from the French by Janet Neis.
U.S. editor: Rita Reitci
Editorial assistant: Diane Laska

Series consultant: Michel Tranier, zoologist at the French National Museum of Natural History.

The editors wish to thank the Jacana Agency, and the artists who kindly granted us permission to use the photographs displayed in the following pages:

Cover, S. Krasemann; 4, J. Robert, K. Ross; 5, J. L. Lemoigne; 6, A. Saunier; 7, J. Robert, J.-M. Labat; 8, K. Ross, J.-M. Labat; 9, Ferrero-Labat; 10, F. Winner; 11, Rouxaine; 12, P. Lorne, Rouxaine; 13, C. Nardin; 14, Y. Arthus-Bertrand; 15, Anup-Shah; 16, C. and M. Moiton; 17, R. Dulhoste, P. Lorne; 18, P. Lorne; 19, P. Summ; 20, J.-P. Varin, Varin-Visage; 21, A. Ducrot; 22, K. Ross; 23, A. Degré, Y. Arthus-Bertrand; 24, F. Gohier; 25, S. De Wilde, Casino; 26, P. Laboute; 27, J.-M. Bassot; 28, Hellio-Van Ingen; 29, G. Pillods; 30, J.-M. Labat; 31, S. Cordier; 32, G. Renson, M. Denis-Huot; 33, E. Dragesco; 34, Varin-Visage; 35, Y. Arthus-Bertrand; 36, Anup-Shah; 37, J.-P. Herny; 38, F. Winner; 39, Frédéric; 40, F. Go; 41, 42, K. Amsler, Varin-Visage; 42, The Museum of Man/P. Colombel; 43, Y. Gladu; 44, Boulay-Caraisco; 45, M. Garnier, S. Cordier

Printed in the United States of America

1 2 3 4 5 6 7 8 9 02 01 00 99 98

CONTENTS

THE NEED FOR NOURISHMENT

Above: **The koala lives entirely on eucalyptus leaves.**

The cell is the smallest unit of life. Animals and plants are composed of cells, from only one to millions of these tiny, basic living units.

Growth occurs when the number of cells increases. However, cells do get old and must be replaced after a while.

In order to function and multiply, cells need energy. This energy must come from the outside, usually as food.

Plants use sunlight to make organic matter out of non-organic materials found in soil, such as water and mineral salts, as well as the carbon dioxide they get from the air. This process is called photosynthesis.

Food for animals

Animals cannot make the organic matter that their cells need. Instead, they must use the matter made by other living cells. This means they must eat it in some form, either as plants or other animals.

Food variety

Many animals eat plants — leaves, roots, fruits, or grain. These animals are called herbivores.

Other animals, called insectivores, live on a diet of insects. Animals called

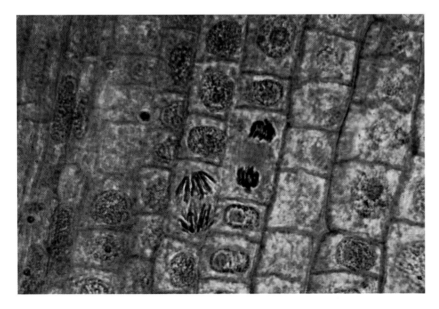

Left: **A hyacinth root seen under a microscope. The cells are rectangular. The ones where chromosomes appear (the dark sticks) are multiplying.**

carnivores hunt down and kill other animals so they can eat their flesh.

A diet, more or less

Some animals will eat only one kind of plant, as the white cabbage butterfly does. The koala eats only eucalyptus leaves, and the endangered panda eats nothing but bamboo shoots.

If the food of these diet specialists becomes scarce in their environments, these animals easily can become extinct.

Gulls eat fish and are willing to dig through trash dumps in their search for food. This allows them to live far from the water. Ravens will eat anything, dead or alive, in order to survive.

Above: **Gulls dig through garbage to find food.**

DIFFERENT FORMS OF NUTRIENTS

Animals that appear similar may seek food in very different forms: grains and seeds for the goldfinch, fruit for the thrush, insects for the swallow, or mammals for the falcon.

Nutritional elements

The cells that make up the bodies of all animals actually are built from the same elements. Only the proportion varies among different species and the different organs, such as muscle, blood, and bone.

No matter what kind of food they eat, all animals need certain kinds of nutritional substances called nutrients. To keep their cells alive and healthy, animals need:

• glucose, with rapid absorption (sugars) or with slow absorption (starches); these exist in the sap or the cellulose of plants, in fruits and grains, in the shells of crustaceans or insects, in vertebrate blood, or in the milk female mammals feed to their young;

• lipids (fats), found in some seeds (sunflower seeds, nuts) and in meat; the livers of many animals can turn excess sugars into fat;

• proteins, found in many cereal grains (wheat, rice, oats, corn), in legumes (peas, beans), and in animal flesh, eggs, and milk;

• vitamins and minerals, which are dissolved in water and contained in plant and animal cells;

• water, which is needed to circulate nutrients through the body's cells; water is supplied by drinking or by eating animals or plants that contain water.

Below: **The thrush likes fruit, but it also will eat worms and insects.**

Left: **A lion at a water hole. Water is as necessary as food.**

Below: **This peregrine falcon has killed a pigeon for food.**

The dietary needs for each species depends on many conditions:
- the food supply in its environment; an animal that eats nothing but wood, for example, can survive only in places where trees grow;
- the ability to obtain and absorb the needed food; the wood-eating animal must be able to gnaw and swallow wood;
- the ability to digest and assimilate the food; the wood-eater's digestive system must be able to dissolve the wood and change cellulose (main part of plant's cell wall) into glucose (sugar).

WAYS OF SWALLOWING FOOD

Above: **The butterfly unrolls its proboscis to suck nectar from flowers.**

Below: **The ground beetle's powerful jaws crush its food.**

The diet of an animal depends on what it can capture and swallow.

Scientists group animals according to the shape of the mouth or jaw.

Among insects, such groups include:
- grinders (such as the cricket), which can tear with their jaws;
- suckers (such as the butterfly), which can only suck up fluids with their soft proboscis;
- lickers (such as the bee), which can swallow thick liquids like honey; and
- stingers (such as the flea, the mosquito, or the cicada), which can use their hard proboscis to pierce skin.

Among birds, the shape of the beak determines the kind of food.

Some beak types are:
- the short, strong beaks of granivores (birds that eat grains and nuts);
- the short, pointed beaks of insectivores; and
- the hooked beaks of birds of prey, which can tear flesh.

Among mammals, the teeth determine the kind of food for:
- carnivores, which have strong canine teeth and cutting molars capable of tearing flesh and grinding bones, and
- herbivores, which have strong incisors that allow them to cut plants, and large, flat molars that crush the plants into pulp.

Changing diets

Caterpillars get food by grinding up leaves. Later they become butterflies that use a proboscis to suck nectar, a sugary juice, from flowers.

Mosquito larvae live in water and eat tiny bits of plants. However, the adult female mosquito pierces the skin of birds and mammals to suck some of their blood.

The tadpole uses its horned mouth to scrape algae from the bottom of its watery home, but when it becomes a frog, it eats mostly insects.

These changes in diet often are due to changes in the digestive system or the shape of the mouth.

Young mammals that are not yet able to feed themselves begin life by drinking their mothers' milk. When their teeth develop, the diet of these young changes to the food habits of their species, eating plants, insects, or other animals.

Below: **This yawning lion shows its teeth, especially its powerful canines.**

AQUATIC AND UNDERGROUND HERBIVORES

Above: **Through the aquarium glass, the Lymnaea, a small freshwater snail, shows its rough tongue behind its open mouth, which allows it to eat plants.**

Filter feeders

Sponges, corals, and mollusks with shells in two parts (bivalves) get their food by taking in the surrounding water.

For food, they filter out the plankton (algae and microscopic animals) that they find in it. The water is sent back outside.

Aquatic plants

The periwinkle, a small sea snail, eats plants with its rasping tongue.

The sea urchin grinds plants from the bottom of the sea.

Many herbivores live in freshwater. These may include snails, such as the great pond snail, or insects, such as the scavenger beetle. Tadpoles and mosquito larvae are also herbivores.

Plants are only a small part of most fish diets. Much of what they eat is animal matter.

Underground eaters

The earthworm eats humus, the decomposed plant matter that makes up the fertile layer of soil. This burrowing worm swallows the earth it finds in front of it, then digests what it can use as food and excretes the rest. The earthworm's tunnels can aerate their home soil.

The mole cricket travels through its underground rooms and gnaws the roots it finds there.

Many larvae that live under ground, such as maybug larvae, also gnaw roots. This can cause damage to plants. Other insects, such as the termite, chew and eat wood.

Below: **The mole cricket digs underground rooms with its powerful front feet.**

VEGETARIAN INVERTEBRATES AND BIRDS

Right: **Aphids suck the sap from a plant. Ants lick the aphids to get their honeydew. A ladybug larva is coming to eat the aphids.**

Below: **A caterpillar eats a cabbage leaf.**

Small leaf-eaters

Before it turns into a butterfly, the caterpillar eats large quantities of plants. Its body is soft, but it possesses a hard, crushing mouth that cuts leaves easily.

Huge swarms of locusts (migratory grasshoppers) can sometimes swoop down onto fields. These hungry insects strip and devour nearly all the vegetation in their path, including crops.

Land slugs and snails also eat leaves and stalks.

Sucking juice

The aphid pierces the leaves and stems of its favorite plants and sucks out the sap. The amount taken would hardly be noticeable if the aphid did not live with hundreds of other aphids.

Aphids also can secrete honeydew, a sweet liquid ants like to drink. Ants stroke aphids to increase the amount of honeydew they produce. The larvae of the ladybug are more interested in eating the aphids themselves.

The cicada larva has a hard proboscis and can pierce tree branches to get sap. The butterfly has a very soft coiled proboscis that it unrolls to suck nectar.

Bees carry most of the nectar they gather in the field back to the beehive, where it is stored and later concentrated to make honey.

Vegetarian birds

The goldfinch likes to eat thistle seeds. The pigeon and the chicken eat mostly grains, so they are called granivores. The sparrow is also a granivore, but it adds insects to its menu.

Some birds that live in warm climates, such as the colorful parrot and the parakeet, have a large, hard beak. They use this beak to break open the hardest seeds.

The blackbird and the thrush like wild berries and fruit.

The hummingbird uses its very thin beak and long tongue to reach deep into the center of a flower and sip the nectar.

Above: **Digging in thistle flowers for seeds, the European goldfinch has stained the feathers around its beak!**

13

HERBIVOROUS MAMMALS

Above: **This squirrel finds plenty of wild nuts to eat.**

grow on trees, such as acorns, hazelnuts, and chestnuts. It can use its front feet to grab food.

Other gnawers, such as the dormouse, prefer to eat fruit. The beaver likes to eat bark and can cut down a tree by gnawing at the base.

The house mouse and field mouse readily help themselves to the food stores of humans. This can be dangerous for these mice if the humans trap them!

Gnawers nibble

The rabbit nibbles in little bites with its long front teeth, or incisors, which never wear out because they always keep on growing.

Similar animals, called gnawers, also nibble, but not always on leaves. The squirrel likes nuts that

Grass-eaters

Grazing sheep snip off the tops of grasses and other vegetation. Wild horses eat grass with seed heads. Cows do not have upper teeth, so they use their hardened gums to tear out tufts of grass. Goats graze as the sheep do, but they also eat branches, with or without leaves, which can damage the plant.

Other plant-eaters

In temperate forests, deer eat leaves and nuts. Wild boars dig for roots. In cold northern steppes, reindeer graze on lichens when grass is scarce. In tropical areas, gazelles and antelopes graze on savanna grass.

Large hippopotamuses eat plants from the water and nearby grasslands. Elephants pull leaves off of trees with their long, flexible trunk and put them into their mouth. Giraffes reach tree leaves with their long neck. They also graze on grass.

Below: **Besides eating tree leaves, the giraffe also grazes. To lower its head far enough to reach the grass, it must spread its front legs.**

INSECTS EATING INSECTS

Above: **This praying mantis devours a grasshopper it has caught.**

Dragonfly and wasp

The dragonfly catches flies, bees, and even other kinds of dragonflies in midair. But it also can remain perched, taking flight only when prey comes within reach.

The wasp, although it likes to eat fruit, also kills insects. Some wasps use their venom to paralyze caterpillars and then lay eggs in the body. When the eggs hatch, the larvae have fresh food at hand.

Praying mantis

The praying mantis gets its name from the way it holds its front legs, which are pincers edged with spines. They are folded up under its body, so the mantis looks as if it is praying. Actually, it is waiting for prey. As soon as an insect comes near, the mantis throws out its legs and closes them like tongs on the prey, which the mantis then devours.

Ant lion larva

The larva of the ant lion makes a trap to catch prey by digging a funnel-shaped hole in dry sand.

Using its head as a shovel, it throws sand outside. It stays hidden at the bottom of the trap with its jaws sticking out. When an ant reaches the pit's edge, shifting sand carries the insect to the bottom. The larva grabs it with its venomous jaws and sucks the juices of its prey. Later, it discards the empty body.

Above: **This ant lion larva has not yet dug its trap. It uses its hook-like jaws to grab ants.**

Right: **A close-up view of a wasp.**

17

OTHER INSECT HUNTERS

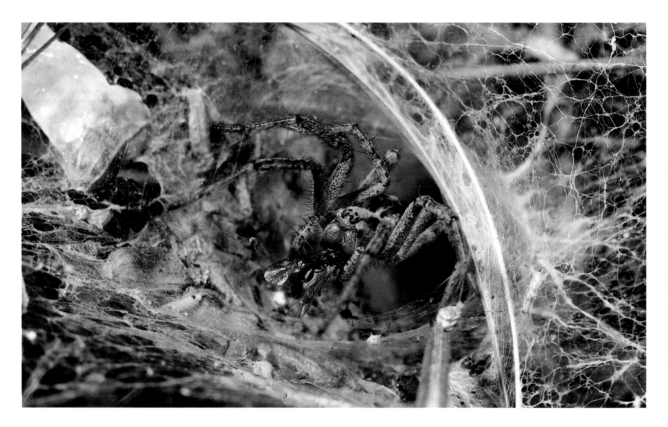

Above: **A spider devours an insect caught in its labyrinth-like web.**

Web traps

Most spiders spin webs with the silk from special glands, called spinnerets, in their abdomen.

The garden spider spins its web between the stalks of plants. When an insect gets stuck in the web, the spider wraps it up with strands of silk. Then, it sucks out the juices from the prey and throws away the empty body.

Other kinds of spiders use their webs differently; for example, dropping a web into the path of their prey or spreading a web on the surface of water to catch insects.

Echo hunting

When it hunts at night, the bat, a small flying mammal, uses echoes to find the insects it eats. The bat makes sharp and piercing cries as it flies, then receives the echoes with its large ears.

This method helps the bat to find prey and also to avoid obstacles that may be in its path.

Sling and lasso

Frogs and toads have a tongue attached at the front of their mouth. When an insect passes by, they quickly sling out their tongue to catch it. Prey sticks to the slimy tongue until the hunter is ready to swallow it. Lizards also can hunt by swiftly thrusting out the tongue to grab prey.

The fastest tongue is owned by the chameleon, known as the lizard that can change colors. It can shoot out a tongue that is longer than its body. The sticky tip can catch insects up to 5 inches (12 centimeters) away.

Below: **The chameleon can shoot out its long tongue to catch insects.**

19

INSECTIVORE BIRDS AND MAMMALS

On the wing

Birds that catch insects while flying usually have a large mouth with a hook at the end of their beak.

Flying through the air, the swallow opens its beak wide and flies into a thick cloud of midges. It also chases insects one by one. The nighthawk and the swift hunt in the same way.

The titmouse, like many other small birds, hunts caterpillars and insects resting on plants.

Above: **As soon as it sees a flying insect, the swallow opens its beak to catch it.**

Right: **The giant anteater thrusts its tongue into tiny cracks to catch ants and termites. These animals live in Central and South America.**

Harpoon tongue

The woodpecker eats insects that live in the bark of trees. It taps its beak on the tree until it makes a hole and finds an insect's hiding place. It then stabs the prey with the horny tip of its long tongue and pulls it out of the hole.

Insectivorous mammals

Besides insects, the hedgehog and the mole eat worms and snails. The hedgehog even will attack vipers because it does not fear the venom of these snakes.

The pangolin, or scaly anteater, eats mostly ants. The aardvark, which is an African anteater, eats ants and termites. Pangolins and anteaters do not feel the bites of their prey.

The aardvark recognizes the scent of its prey's nest and tears the nest apart with its claws. Then it sticks in its long, slimy tongue so that over a hundred ants or termites can get stuck to it. The anteater can swallow thousands of ants or termites in one meal.

The badger likes to hunt insects, but it also eats earthworms and honey. The shrew eats mostly insects. It needs to eat two-thirds of its total body weight every day.

Above: **A woodpecker drilling a hole in a tree trunk.**

BLOODSUCKERS AND CARRION EATERS

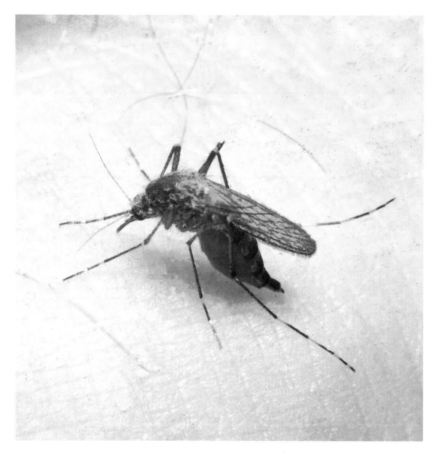

Above: **This female mosquito's abdomen swells up from the blood she drinks.**

Sippers

Instead of hunting and killing other creatures, some small animals suck blood — which is a very nourishing substance — from other animals.

A well-known example is the mosquito. Only the female mosquito bites; she needs blood so that her eggs can hatch. The flea, the bedbug, and certain flies also drink blood from their victims.

The vampire bat of South America gently bites and licks the blood of its prey, usually cows and goats. Normally, the prey doesn't even notice.

The risk to animals is not from the small amount of blood these bats take. The main danger is possible transmission of diseases when these bloodsuckers bite one victim after another. The anopheles mosquito can carry malaria. The African tsetse fly carries sleeping sickness.

Carrion feeders

Some animals feed on decaying carcasses, which may have been partly eaten by other animals. We call animals that eat this way carrion feeders.

Green flies eat rotting or decomposing meat and lay their eggs in it. When the eggs hatch, the larvae, called maggots, eat the food.

Army ants march in columns and will devour anything, even birds and small mammals, that they find in their path.

Vultures often kill sick or frail creatures, but before their weak claws and bill can tear into the prey, it must already have started to decay. Vultures also eat dead animals they find. They can clean up everything, leaving only the skeleton.

Carrion feeders, like the jackal and the hyena, kill prey but also eat other carcasses. Large prey, however, rarely is eaten in one meal. It begins to rot before the predators finish it, so they become accustomed to eating carrion, even carcasses, they find. Lions and tigers also eat carcasses.

Above: **The hyena and the vultures compete for this carcass.**

Below: **The jackals of this pack share a carcass.**

CARNIVORES IN THE WATER

Above: **The whale filters water with its comb-like baleen plates to gather krill.**

Most fish have very small teeth that don't allow them to cut up their food, so they just swallow what they can fit in their mouths. Some species, such as the pike, can open their mouths very wide by elongating them toward the front.

The smallest fish can swallow plankton, eggs, and newly-hatched fish. They themselves become the prey of larger fish, who then become the prey of even larger fish. This chain goes from anchovies up to sharks.

Gulping down

Crustaceans and fish are often carnivores, or they can be omnivores that eat both plant and animal matter. The only limit is the size of the prey that they can swallow.

Crustaceans have small mouths, but jaws outside the mouth help them cut up their food. Some, like the crab and the lobster, also have pincers to help them seize their prey.

Filtering out

The baleen whale has a small gullet and only can swallow tiny shrimp, called krill. Since it must eat millions of krill each day to get enough food, the whale takes in huge quantities of water. Then it forces the water back out through baleen, large plates in its mouth that

act as a sieve. The plates filter out the krill, which the whale swallows.

The chase

Most fish chase their prey. Fish with strong teeth in their jaws can attack large prey, because they can grab them before eating them. Very few freshwater fish can escape the pike's teeth.

Insect predators

Predatory insects live in pond water. The larvae of dragonflies have a long, hinged structure with a pair of claspers that folds back under the face when not in use. It shoots out to catch prey, such as other insects, small fish, or tadpoles.

The dytiscids, or diving beetles, and their larvae target the same kind of prey as dragonfly larvae. The aggressive dytiscid larvae, or water tigers, suck juices from their prey with two hollow, hook-shaped jaws.

Above: **The fierce barracuda catches smaller fish and can attack human divers.**

Below: **Dragonfly larvae can attack small lizards and fish.**

Other Underwater Hunting Methods

Above: **The sea anemone does not sting this clown fish, whose slimy coat picks up the anemone's own scent. The clown fish lures victim fish and eats the leftovers from the anemone's meals.**

The lovely sea anemone resembles a flower, but the "petals" are really venomous tentacles that are similar to those of the jellyfish. These tentacles trap crustaceans or fish that come too close.

The octopus uses its tentacle arms, covered with suckers, to seize its prey of crustaceans or fish. It bites off chunks from its catch with its parrot-like beak.

Prying open

The starfish is not able to swallow the mollusks it eats. So, it pulls on the bivalve with the tubular feet covering its arms, and forces open the shell. Then it pushes just its stomach inside the shell. It doesn't have to go all the way inside the shell to digest the mollusk's flesh. When it has finished its meal, the starfish pulls its full stomach back into its body, leaving the shell.

Animal traps

The jellyfish floats in the sea, trailing behind long tentacles covered with venomous stingers. The tentacles trap prey that the jellyfish will quickly digest.

Some mollusks, such as the cone shell, can make a hole in the shells of other animals to absorb their flesh. Some cone shells can kill fish and injure humans with their poisonous stinger.

Shock and light

Several species of fish, such as the ray and the electric eel, have organs that produce electrical discharges which paralyze their prey.

Some fish that live in deep, dark water have shiny spots on their heads to attract prey. The fish swallow the prey when it nears the light.

Prey in the air

Many fish, such as the trout, catch insects that fly over the surface of the water. Often, they stick their heads out of the water to do this. The archer fish spits jets of water at insects that fly within its range. Then it swallows the insects that fall into the water.

The crocodile swims just under the water's surface, with only its eyes and nostrils above the water. When prey comes to drink, the crocodile drags it into the water to drown it. The crocodile will eat it a little later.

Below: **This fish lives in deep, dark water, where its shiny scales attract prey.**

FISHING BIRDS

Above: **This heron has just caught a fish.**

Fish on foot

Waders are birds that have long legs that they use for walking slowly, or wading, in shallow water.

The flamingo roots in the mud of the water bottom. It uses its beak to filter out algae and the small crustaceans that give its feathers their beautiful pink color.

The heron hunts fish. It prefers eels, but it also will eat frogs and some species of insects.

On the beach, some birds dig in the sand for the mollusks and worms that are buried there.

Fishing in flight

The osprey, a bird of prey, dives toward the water, thrusting its talons under the surface to grab a fish. It returns to dry land to eat its prey.

To catch a meal, the brown pelican dives into water, scooping fish and water into the expanding pouch on its lower beak. It spills the water out and swallows the fish.

Chasing fish

Some pelicans swim in groups, herding fish into shallow water where they can scoop them up easily.

The gannet will dive completely under water to catch fish to eat.

Some penguins use their wings for swimming under water when they are chasing fish.

The kingfisher perches on a tree at the river's edge and watches for fish to swim by. Suddenly, it dives on its prey, grabs it, and returns to its perch. The bird swallows its prey head first so the fins will fold back and not stick in its throat.

FISHING MAMMALS

Above: **The otter leaves the water to eat the fish it caught.**

The otter dives and swims in rivers to catch fish, then climbs on a rock to devour its meal.

The grizzly bear likes salmon from the river, but since its paws are too large to grab them, it must use another fishing technique. Sweeping its paw through the water, the bear scoops the fish out of the stream. It then can pick its prey up in its teeth. When the salmon leap up waterfalls, the bear can catch them in its jaws.

Polar hunters

The killer whale is a sea mammal about 33 feet (10 m) long. It feeds mostly on seals. Hunting in groups, these animals circle their prey. One hunting trick is to tip over the block of ice where a seal is resting and then grab the seal.

The sea leopard is a large Antarctic seal that likes to eat penguins, but these birds can outswim it. So the sea leopard hides under ice floes, and it catches the penguins as they dive from the floes into the water.

The polar bear swims under the water, allowing only its eyes and nostrils to appear above the water's surface. In this way, it can sneak up and grab ducks as they rest on the water.

The polar bear also eats baby seals. It has learned to find their homes by watching the comings and goings of the mother seals. The bear will break through a home's icy roof and grab a baby seal.

Below: **This Alaskan grizzly bear catches a tasty salmon.**

CARNIVOROUS REPTILES AND BIRDS

Open wide

Some snakes, such as the python and the boa, suffocate their prey by tightly wrapping their body around it so it is unable to breathe.

Other snakes, such as the viper and the cobra, paralyze or kill their prey with a bite that injects it with poison.

The grass snake eats small rodents and frogs. Sometimes it even eats birds' eggs.

Because snakes cannot cut up or chew their prey, they must swallow their catch whole. They can open their jaws very wide by separating them at the joint. Sometimes a snake needs several hours to swallow the prey, and it may need several days to

Above: **The python suffocates a gazelle by circling its body.**

Left: **The python swallows its prey whole.**

digest it. The snake cannot move easily during this time because its body is swollen by the animal it has swallowed.

Birds of prey

The buzzard flies over its territory. When it sees a small rodent, it swoops down to catch and eat it.

The owl hunts at night. It flies silently, which allows it to sneak up even on prey that hear well.

The eagle dives head first toward an animal, often a rabbit. When near its prey, the bird brakes and grabs the prey with its talons, killing it. Then the eagle takes it back to its nest. Because it will feed on carcasses, some people think the eagle kills sheep, but this never has been proven.

The falcon eats rabbits and large birds. It, too, dives head first to attack.

Below: **This falcon devours a rabbit.**

CARNIVOROUS LAND MAMMALS

Above: **The tiger sneaks close to its prey before pouncing.**

Below: **The ermine hunts in the burrows of its prey.**

Creeping up

A small cat watches a bird or a mouse, and, crouching low to the ground, it silently creeps up on it. However, the cat won't leap until it is close enough to strike the prey with its claws.

The tiger hunts in much the same way. It sneaks through the grasses of the jungle, waiting for just the right moment to snatch its prey, usually grabbing it by the throat.

Invading

The ermine invades mole holes and rabbit burrows. It bites the base of the skull and neck of its prey, which cannot escape in time. The marten hunts in the nests of birds or squirrels. It also eats rabbits and fruit.

Hunting in groups

Many predators like to hunt in packs, so that they easily can surround their

Chasing down

A dog catches its prey by chasing after it. The greyhound is fastest of all the dogs. It can catch a running rabbit.

The cheetah is the fastest hunter on land. It cannot run long distances without getting tired, but the cheetah can catch any of the hoofed animals, even a gazelle.

prey. They usually cut one animal out of the herd, then attack it on several sides so it has no chance of escape. Lions hunt this way.

The female lions, or lionesses, do the hunting, but the male lions still take the first and best part of the feast.

Wolves, jackals, and hyenas also hunt in packs.

Varied diet

The red fox eats a large number of insects in the summer. But, mostly, it eats field mice. It also might catch a rabbit occasionally, and when it finds a poultry yard it can get into, the fox will catch a chicken to feed its family. The red fox also will eat carrion, grass, and fruit.

Below: **These lionesses separated their prey from the herd so they can kill it.**

DIGESTING FOOD

Above: **The tiger has caught its prey and begins eating its meal.**

Long and short tracts

Food is broken down in the digestive tract, which begins at the mouth and ends at the anus, where waste is expelled in the form of droppings.

Carnivorous animals have a shorter digestive tract than herbivores. The cow's intestine, for example, is five times longer than the lion's tract. This size difference is necessary because plant fiber is more difficult to break down than animal flesh, and so it needs to stay longer inside the digestive tract.

Catching and eating food is only the start of nourishment. In order to carry energy to billions of cells in an animal's body, food must be digested. This process breaks food down into nutrients that are dissolved in the blood and carried throughout the body.

Digestive action

To help digestion, many internal glands secrete liquids that can dissolve or break down food.

Saliva in an animal's mouth begins to break down food even before it has been swallowed.

Through the digestive tract, other secretions act

to help break down food into particles that the body can assimilate.

Snakes have powerful digestive juices that can dissolve the bones of prey that they have swallowed whole. Birds of prey are unable to dissolve animal bones. Instead, they spit them up as pellets.

The role of bacteria

In the digestive system, microscopic, one-celled organisms called bacteria play an important part in breaking down food into nutrients. Some bacteria break down the cellulose of plants into sugars.

When this portion of the digestive process ends, nutrients pass into the blood, which then carries them throughout the body to feed the cells.

Some kinds of bacteria are necessary to animals. Other kinds of bacteria can cause illness or even the deaths of animals.

Right: **The giraffe digests its food with the help of bacteria.**

A More Complete Digestion

Above: **Termites feed one another.**

come back up into the animal's mouth. The animal chews the cud to mix in some more saliva, and swallows it again. This time the food passes through other sections of the stomach to complete its digestion.

This fermentation takes place in the rabbit just before the material gets to the anus. This is too late for nutrients to pass into the blood. So the rabbit must eat its soft droppings, which are not waste, but fermented plant food. In a second digestion, the nutrients go into the blood and only waste is excreted.

Two-step digestion

Ruminating animals such as the cow, the deer, and the camel, begin digestion in the rumen, the first pouch of the stomach. Bacteria start to break down the plants that were eaten. Then, balls of fermented plant paste, called the cud,

Nourishing others

In termites, wood is broken down into its nutrients by bacteria in the insect's digestive tract and by a fungus grown and eaten by these insects. This digestion happens too quickly to allow full

absorption. So the termites must feed each other a nutritious liquid that is the final product of their digestion. This method of feeding is possible because termites live in large communities.

Easy-to-digest food

Female mammals have mammary glands from which they secrete milk to nourish their young.

The pigeon feeds its chicks a white liquid that it secretes from its crop.

The young of some sea birds dig into the throats of their parents to get a paste of partly-digested fish to eat.

Above: **The camel ruminates the same way the cow does.**

Right: **This pelican feeds its young by letting it dig fish from its throat.**

THE FOOD CHAIN

Below: **A diagram of one food chain.**

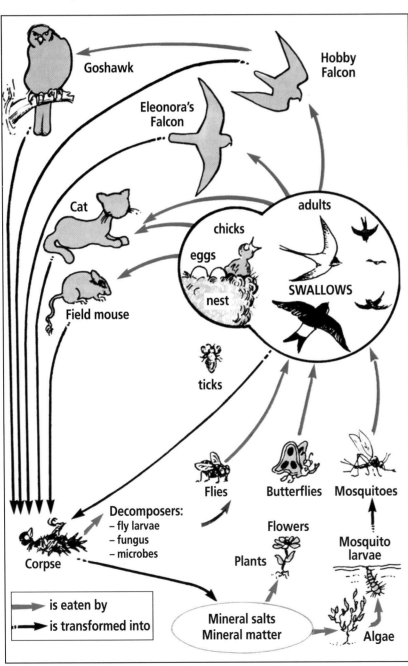

Goshawk

Hobby Falcon

Eleonora's Falcon

Cat

adults

chicks

eggs

SWALLOWS

nest

Field mouse

ticks

Flies

Butterflies

Mosquitoes

Decomposers:
– fly larvae
– fungus
– microbes

Flowers

Mosquito larvae

Corpse

Plants

→ is eaten by

--→ is transformed into

Mineral salts
Mineral matter

Algae

Plants are the real food producers. Animals are only consumers of the plants or of plant-eaters.

The links between many animals, where each eats and then is eaten, make up what is called a food chain. Some animals are eaten only after they die, by bacteria, maggots, or carrion feeders. This is part of the food chain.

Below: **The titmouse, predator of the worm, may become the prey of a fox.**

Passing it on

Each animal in the food chain passes only a small part (about 10%) of the food it gets to the next animal. It uses the rest for its own daily energy requirements. To gain 3.5 ounces (100 grams), an animal must eat 2.2 pounds (1 kilogram) of fish. A fish that weighs 2.2 pounds (1 kg) must eat 22 pounds (10 kg) of small animals, or zooplankton. These, in turn, must eat about 220 pounds (100 kg) of phytoplankton, which is living matter that is made by photosynthesis.

This food chain shows how important plants are to all animals, including humans, for survival. By destroying plant habitats, humans also destroy the natural food chain that feeds them.

Above: **The great white shark is a super predator at the top of its food chain.**

Below: **The fox can become the prey of a bird of prey.**

ECOLOGICAL BALANCE

The drawings found on rocks in the Sahara *(above)* show that this desert once was like the landscape *(below)* now found much farther south.

The food chain depends on ecological balance.

If the climate allows plenty of plant growth, the first consumers — herbivores — will feed well and will multiply. Then their predators will have more food to eat and also will multiply.

If plants become scarce in a region, herbivorous animals will find little food and will decrease in number. Their predators, also having less food, will start to disappear.

When plants no longer are able to survive, their extinction also brings about the extinction of the animals of that area. Prehistoric carvings from about 7,000 years ago on some rocks in the Sahara

show giraffes, rhinoceroses, and hippopotamuses in places that are now arid deserts.

This shows why we must protect the forests and grasslands and also prevent the pollution of the rivers and seas that support all life.

Concentration

The food chain acts as a pyramid, concentrating toxins, or poisons, at the top. The first consumers don't take in enough of the toxins to kill them.

But animals eating them consume the toxins these plants or animals have stored in their bodies.

For example, in the summer, poisonous algae and bacteria develop in the sea. Scallops can eat them safely, but the humans who then eat the scallops, which have eaten the bacteria and algae, can be poisoned.

About twenty years ago, in Japan's Minamata Bay, over 100 people were poisoned by mercury salts that were dumped into

Above: **The scarcity of plant life in this Mexican desert means fewer animals can live here.**

the sea by a factory. Each animal that ate toxic prey stored up more mercury. The people ate toxic fish.

The same concentration can occur with pesticides or radioactive particles. After the accident at the Chernobyl nuclear power plant in the Ukraine, high levels of radioactive particles were stored up by plants and animals.

UPSETTING THE BALANCE

Above: **Dinosaurs exist today only as fossils, such as the one reconstructed here. This maiasaurus, shown with its eggs and a newly-hatched young, was about 30 feet (9 m) long.**

Sometimes a natural phenomenon, such as the landing of a meteorite, a change of climate, or a volcanic eruption, causes an ecological upheaval. This kind of disruption is probably how all the dinosaurs, including the most enormous, became extinct within the same time period.

Now, humans are the principal cause of drastic ecological disturbances. By clearing away the forests and drying up wetlands, people destroy the homes of many plants and animals.

By not controlling the development of cities or the pollution caused by many industries, humans are bringing about the destruction of nature.

By overfishing and by killing migrating birds, such as the European ringdove, humans risk the extinction of these species by reducing the numbers that reproduce.

In destroying massive quantities of insect pests with chemicals, humans also kill useful insects, such as bees, which help pollinate food crops and other plants so they will reproduce. This poisons, too, the birds that eat the insects, and, then, the predators of those birds.

Plants, animals, and humans, which are at the top of the food chain, face the greatest danger.

Restoring balance

People have begun to protect and restore the ecological balance by establishing some natural preserves of mountains, forests, and wetlands.

In some places, people are reintroducing the predators to help restore balance to those areas. For example, restoring wolves will help prevent the overpopulation of destructive herbivores in a forest.

In order to kill insect pests, biological controls can be used instead of harmful chemicals. For example, ladybugs can be used to control aphids.

Laws and regulations limit the use of harsh chemicals in agriculture and help reduce pollution in cities and industries. Laws also can reduce the

use of energy — one cause of global warming — which can lead to changes in climate.

These efforts and others can increase the chances that all living species, including humans, will survive. But everyone must be prepared to do his or her part.

Right: **Many hunters refuse to believe that they endanger migrating birds.**

Below: **These rabbits killed in France illustrate the waste of unlimited hunting.**

GLOSSARY

aerate — to allow air into a place or substance.

algae — plants that live in water and have no roots, stems, or leaves.

assimilate — to absorb nourishment into the system.

bacteria — single-celled, microscopic organisms.

canine teeth — sharp, pointed teeth, or fangs, in front of an animal's mouth, for tearing off meat or tough food.

carnivores — animals that kill and eat other animals.

cell — the smallest unit of life that can exist independently.

decompose — to decay or gradually break down.

ecological balance — the relationships of living things with their environments.

environment — the surroundings in which plants, animals, and other organisms live.

excrete — to expel waste from the body of an animal.

filter (*v*) — to remove something from a liquid by passing it through a structure.

glucose — sugars occurring widely in plants and easily absorbed as food by animals.

granivores — animals that eat only grains, including nuts.

herbivores — animals that eat only plants.

incisors — sharp teeth in the center front of an animal's mouth, used for cutting.

insectivores — animals that eat only insects.

larva (*pl* larvae) — the wingless, wormlike form of a newly-hatched insect; the stage of life after the egg but before full development.

lipids — various types of fats in nature, often consumed by animals as food.

mammals — warm-blooded vertebrates with hair that give birth to live young and feed them milk from their bodies.

molars — the cheek teeth of mammals behind the incisors and canines, often flat and used for grinding food.

nectar — a sweet liquid found in many flowers that is often used as food by insects.

nutrients — the elements in food that help a plant or animal grow and develop.

omnivores — animals that eat both meat and plants.

organic matter — matter that makes up plants and animals.

photosynthesis — the process by which plants use sunlight to turn minerals, carbon dioxide, and water into organic matter, such as food.

plankton — tiny plants and animals that drift in the oceans, lakes, and rivers.

proboscis — the long feeding tube, or tongue, located on the head of some insects.

proteins — the essential nitrogen-containing part of all living cells; the flesh of animals is largely protein.

savannah — a flat landscape or plain, usually covered with grasses and scattered trees.

steppe — a vast, level plain, usually without trees.

tadpole — the larva of a frog or toad.

temperate — belonging to climate zones with warm summers and cold winters that lie between the tropics and the polar regions.

tropical — belonging to the tropics, or the region centered on the equator and lying between the Tropic of Cancer (23.5° north of the equator) and the Tropic of Capricorn (23.5° south of the equator). This region is typically very hot and humid.

venom — poison secreted by some animals, such as snakes and spiders.

BOOKS TO READ

Animal Families series. (Gareth Stevens)

Animal Magic series. (Gareth Stevens)

Discovering Marine Mammals. Nancy Field and Sally Machlis (Dog Eared Publications)

ENDANGERED! series. Bob Burton (Gareth Stevens)

Frogs, Toads, Lizards and Salamanders. Nancy W. Parker & Joan R. Wright (Morrow)

Great Predators of the Land. Querida L. Pierce (Tor Books)

In Peril series. Barbara J. Behm and Jean-Christophe Balouet (Gareth Stevens)

Life in the Oceans. Lucy Baker (Scholastic)

The Living World. Roger Cleeve (Silver Burdett Press)

Mammals. Jenny Tesar (Blackbirch)

The New Creepy Crawly Collection series. (Gareth Stevens)

Secrets of the Animal World series. (Gareth Stevens)

Surprising Swimmers. Anthony D. Fredericks (NorthWord)

Wonderful World of Animals series. Beatrice MacLeod (Gareth Stevens)

VIDEOS

Animal Predators and the Balance of Nature. (Altschul Group)

Animals Eat in Many Ways. (Phoenix/BFA Film and Video)

Birds & Their Young. (International Film Bureau)

How and What Animals Eat. (Agency for Instructional Technology)

Insects: Little Giants of the Earth. (Coronet)

WEB SITES

www.dolphin-institute.com/dolphins/fourstarframe.html

www.pelagic.org/index.html

http://frog.simplenet.com/froggy/

http://north.audubon.org/

INDEX